THE ULTIMATE WEDDING DANCE

Personal Copy of

Mr. & Mrs.

___

The Ultimate Wedding Dance
Copyright © 2020 by Daniel Buhala

All Rights Reserved. This book or any portion thereof may not be reproduced, distributed or transmitted in any form or by any means, including photocopying, recording, or other electronic or mechanical methods, without the prior written permission of the publisher, except in case of brief quotations embodied in critical reviews and certain other noncommercial uses permitted by copyright law. For permission requests, write to the publisher, addressed "Attention: Permissions Coordinator," at the address below or e-mail: info@dancesportartstudios.com

Although the author and publisher have made every effort to ensure that the information in this book was correct at press time, the author and publisher do not assume and hereby disclaim any liability to any party for any loss, damage, or disruption caused by errors or omissions, whether such errors or omissions result from negligence, accident, or any other cause.

Names, characters, businesses, places, events, locales, and incidents are either the products of the author's imagination or used in a fictitious manner. Any resemblance to actual persons, living or dead, or actual events is purely coincidental.

Paperback: ISBN 978-1-7359000-1-8
Hardcover: ISBN 978-1-7359000-2-5
E-book: ISBN 978-1-7359000-4-9

First Edition: October 2020

Cover art by Yevgenia Rogatina
All Photographs by Amber Holley
Book Design by Marko Markovic (fiverr.com/5mediadesign)

Printed and bound in the United States of America
First printing October 2020

Dance Art Studios Inc/Dance Art Press
PO Box 27879
Los Angeles, Ca 90027

www.theultimateweddingdance.com

*To my grandma and grandpa for
their love, goodness and care.*

*Babke a dedkovi, za ich lásku,
dobrotu a sarostlivosť.*

Wedding Dance?" My response is always the same: "Yes I do, when is your wedding?"

Over the years, the wedding couples whom I have taught and choreographed their First Dance have regularly reached out to me after their wedding and shared their appreciation for all that I prepared them for - on their special day. This includes the choreography of the dance, but more importantly, the information needed to create a one of a kind Wedding Dance, the details within the preparation and the plan for the day of the wedding that consist of all the logistics, tips and tricks that make the performance extraordinary for the wedding couple and their guests. I'd like to share these details with you, not only to create a Wedding Dance of your dreams, but also to have a joyful experience throughout the process and while performing.

My intention with this book is to help "You" and as many wedding couples in the world as possible. I wrote this book also for the dance teachers, instructors and choreographers, as well as the wedding planners, coordinators and even the venue owners and service providers. I want everyone involved with your wedding planning to have an overall idea about the Wedding Dance and everything that goes with it.

So what should a Wedding Dance be all about? Only two things: First, the journey towards your Wedding Dance should be fun along the way as you look for ideas, putting the choreography together and practicing it; Second, the actual performance of your Wedding Dance should be meaningful, as it allows you to celebrate your new life and share the joy of your relationship with your friends and family.

Cheers
Daniel Buhala

Introduction

*I*n this Ultimate Wedding Dance book, you will find all the information you need to make your Wedding Dance an unforgettable experience. All the chapters, the structure, and how this book is written will give you a very clear idea about the preparation, what you need to know about the choreography, and also the tips and tricks on how to make your journey towards your Wedding Dance a pleasant one. Also if you decide to do it on your own, there is a step by step plan on how to create a wedding dance of your dreams.

Every chapter has a clear objective: ideas, the do's and don'ts, examples, charts, pictures, checklists and space for your notes so you can have all the information you need in the palm of your hand. Use this book as a workbook to write your notes and ideas and fill out the checklists, to make the process of creating your Wedding Dance easier and most of all, fun.

The first thing you need to do before starting this journey is talk to your husband or wife to be, about the Wedding Dance and agree that you both want to make your First Dance at your wedding a very special occasion. This mutual understanding will save you a lot of precious time and discussions along the way and it will make the journey towards your Wedding Dance an unforgettable experience. I wish you dear couple a wonderful time creating your very own Ultimate Wedding Dance.

History of the Wedding Dance

The first dance was originally a tradition used to open a ball or a special event, dating as far back as the 17th century. It was the custom for the guests of honor, typically someone high on the social ladder or even a royal family member, to have the first dance of the evening. Once the first dance was completed, everyone was invited to shake their corsets and powdered wigs on the dance floor. In the days of Kings and Queens, ballroom dancing was a skill and it was a big part of the educational system. As it is with so many traditions, this social norm of old has now evolved into a tradition at our modern-day weddings.

Awareness note

We live in the 21st century and the world recognizes, and is more aware and open about same-sex marriages. Throughout my career as a coach and choreographer, I choreographed many same-sex Wedding Dances. For your understanding, the terminology "The Groom" (leader) and "The Bride" (follower) is used throughout the book. It will simplify the understanding of the different roles in dancing, clarify the learning of steps, movement and which one of you is dancing a particular segment of the choreography. Thank you for your understanding!

Chapter 1

Everything You Need to Know Before You Start

Timeline

As I previously mentioned in the preface, make sure you're on the same page with your fiancé. Check! Now there are other important questions you need to ask yourselves: When is the wedding, months, weeks, perhaps days till the wedding date? Do we want to involve a professional choreographer or create the Wedding Dance ourselves? What should our Wedding Dance look like? Your availability and dedication to practice is a necessary part in this process.

To simplify the process and create a performance that will give your wedding reception the glow and sparkle like the little cute wedding couple on your wedding cake, I will introduce you to the three performance categories you can choose from to make your Wedding Dance amazing and enjoyable. Every category will have a detailed description (what the performance is about), the times (weeks or minimum lessons needed) and examples for convenience.

> **Note:** For those couples who are in a big hurry and there's a lack of time, skip to page 31 and read the section "The Last Minute Recommendations" to ensure that you won't make the same mistakes most couples do when they forget about their First Dance.

on the beach in the Caribbean and your dance floor is full of sand or even the sand itself.

Before creating the choreography of your First Dance, let your dance instructor know about the surface and the size of the space you will dance on (minimum recommended size 20x20 feet) to avoid possible errors. The safest way to dance a worry-free performance is to have an even and smooth surface, ideally a wooden dance floor. Sometimes a venue has no dance floor and one will be installed especially for your event. It is important to communicate with your wedding planner that the venue will need a dance floor and the space is big enough to dance on. These installed floors are slightly elevated and you must be careful when you walk onto it to avoid tripping over the edge.

When you are at the venue discussing and planning the decorations, walk on the floor that you will be dancing on and test how it feels. Is it slippery, sticky, or does it feel just right? This should be done with the actual shoes you plan to dance your First Dance to ensure that you will have a marvelous performance and your guests will have a great time dancing the night away.

The Layout of the Reception Area

The layout of the reception area and where the dance floor is located is of vital importance for your First Dance not only choreographically, but for your guests and audience as well. The main focus here are three things: Where in the ballroom or the venue is the dance floor? On how many sides around the dance floor will you have an audience? Where is your sweetheart table in relation to the dance floor? Here are some examples of possible layouts starting with the most convenient layout for your performance.

Three Sides Audience

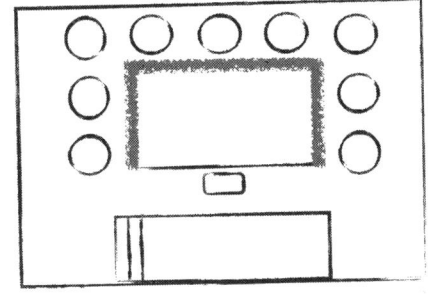

If you are planning your ballroom setup with your wedding coordinator, the ideal setup to perform your wedding dance is definitely the 3 sides layout. This type of layout gives you and your instructor the opportunity to create a rich choreography that your audience will enjoy watching, regardless of where they are sitting. With this arrangement, it is easy to dance the side by side segments of your wedding dance towards your audience without facing the empty side (unless intentionally choreographed).

Four Sides Audience

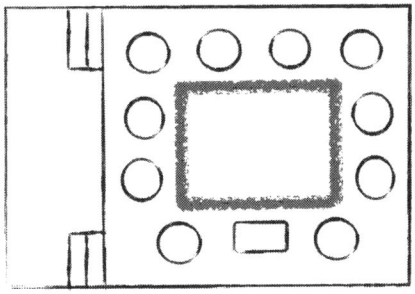

The second possible layout choice would be the 4 sides type. The choreographic content in this type of layout has almost unlimited possibilities and you do not need to worry which way you turn because you have an audience all around you. The only downside of this type of setup is that one side of the audience will always see you from behind while dancing side by side segments of the dance routine.

One Side Audience

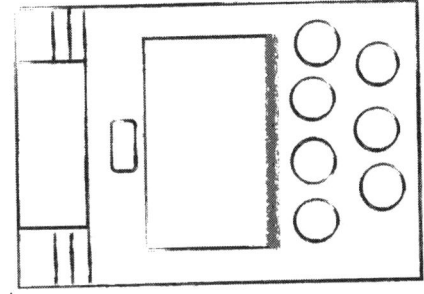

If your audience is seated only on one side of the dance floor, your choreography will be very similar to a theatrical performance that tells your story exclusively facing your audience. To dance and manage the directions within this setup is easy because you know that you need to face your audience for specific parts of your performance, and there is only one side you can face.

Two Sides Audience

There are two types of the two sides audience layouts. The first version is where the audience sides are adjacent to each other "The L Shape" and second variation is "The Mirrored Type" where the audience sides are facing each other.

The L Shape

The L Shape layout is very fitting if your venue has limited space and you are not able to have tables on more than two sides. This type of arrangement is similar to the 3 sides as well as the one side layout and is very beneficial, choreographically speaking. While performing the side by side segments, the direction you are facing will be the corner where the two sides of the audience meet.

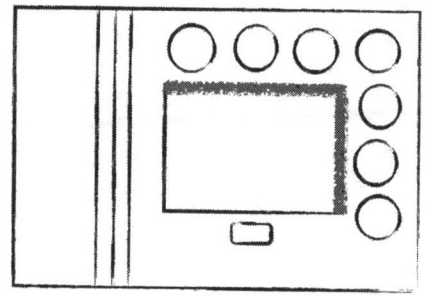

The Mirrored Type

The mirrored type is the least favorable from the choreographic viewpoint. We have a similar issue with the 4 sides type with the difference that when you are facing one half of your guests, the other half will see your back. To choreograph and perform in this setup is very challenging, and it will not be fully satisfying for you or your wedding crowd.

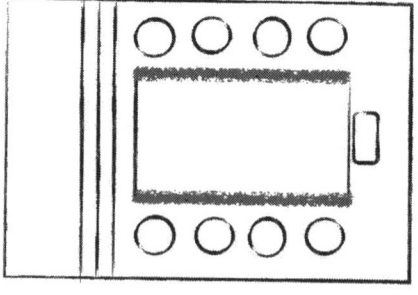

> **Note:** Some venues have the dance floor elevated and set up as a stage, and to enter the dance floor you might often use a couple of stairs. This is usually equal to the layout with the audience on one side but varies and depends on the venue and its setup. Be careful entering and exiting the dance floor because there might be a surface difference. The ballroom surface might be a carpet and the stage space might be a wooden floor.

The Sweetheart Table and Entrance

The position of your sweetheart table and the entrance in relation to the dance floor are relevant for the choreography of your First Dance. The position of these basically dictate how long the beginning of your performance might be, and what it could look like. Your music choice is also a factor. More about this topic in the section "The Choreography" on page 35.

Schedule of the Event

The schedule of the event determines the position of the wedding couple before their First Dance. This is the fundamental key for your choreography and where it starts. Let's look at possible schedule examples:

- Cocktail hour before the reception
- Guests are seated
- Grand entrance (bridal party including the wedding couple)
- <u>First Dance</u>
- Father/Daughter Dance
- Mother/Son Dance

In this schedule example, the First Dance is performed right after the grand entrance. Choreographically speaking, the end of your grand entrance will overlap with the beginning of your Wedding Dance (more about this topic in the section "The Choreography" on page 35). Another schedule example:

- Cocktail hour before the reception
- Guests are seated
- Grand entrance (bridal party including the wedding couple)
- Best Man speech
- <u>First Dance</u>
- Welcome speech (Father of the Bride or Guest of Honor)
- Father/Daughter and Mother/Son performance, danced simultaneously

Here, your Wedding Dance is announced after the Best Man's speech, and the starting position of your choreography will be your sweetheart table.

Thoughts

Some weddings have the First Dance performance scheduled while the guests are eating or even after dinner. I strongly advise you not to do this for a couple of reasons. First, dear Grooms, let's be honest for a second. Your Bride will feel very conscious about the way she looks in her gorgeous wedding dress after dinner. We do not need any other reason, do we? But jokes aside, another reason is your wedding crowd. They will be busy chatting, eating and drinking, and even though they are very polite and they came to celebrate with you, the tasty food takes their senses away for a minute, and that's just a fact. When you are about to perform your Wedding Dance, make sure the crowd has nothing to do other than to watch and enjoy your beautiful performance.

Communicate with your wedding coordinator about the timetable of your event and let your dance instructor know what your schedule looks like before creating your Wedding Dance choreography. Avoid awkward pauses between the scheduled event (the grand entrance, a speech, etc.) before your First Dance and the actual beginning of the performance. How to do this transition smoothly and more about this topic is in the section "The Choreography" on page 35.

Your Wedding Attire

You guessed right! The theme of this section is your gorgeous wedding dress and the Groom's tuxedo (or attire of your choice;

traditional, culturally appropriate, etc.). It is, without a doubt, one of the first things you thought about when your fiancé proposed to you. The Classic, The Surprise Wedding Dance and The Entertainer categories are usually performed in your ceremonial attire. Should you choose The Themed Wedding Dance and decide to have special costumes, be certain to communicate with your wedding coordinator to reserve time for your wardrobe change.

The attention in this section goes to the awareness about the mobility or limitations of your wedding dress and tuxedo. Ladies first!

Bride's Attire

The style of your wedding dress plays a significant role in your First Dance and may affect your choreography. The majority of wedding dresses come with a long and gorgeous train at the back of the dress. When you walk down the aisle towards the "man of your dreams," it gives you an elegant look and great confidence as the train slides gracefully behind you. Simply stunning! Make sure that your wedding gown has the option to pin the train up for your wedding performance (most dresses already have that option, but if not, I'm sure your dress designer will gladly help you with it).

The second thing you need to be aware of and mention to your choreographer beforehand is the skirt style of your wedding dress: will it be tailored around your thighs (this style might limit the length of your steps), or will it have volume (you might have a wire or a petticoat underneath), which makes it more challenging to dance in your dress and your wedding routine must be choreographed accordingly.

And, last but not least, the upper part of your wedding dress can have many possible designs: a beautiful strapless ballgown, a sheath style dress with straps around your arms, a mermaid style dress with a closed top and open back with long sleeves, and more. When fitting your dress, give it a twirl, feel how it moves. Try to raise yours arms and note how freely you can move them. Your choreography may have underarm turns and other interesting dance moves where you may need to raise your arms. If you are limited with your arm movements, show your instructor the photo of your dress (but be careful don't let your fiancé see it!) so your Wedding Dance can be choreographed accordingly.

All points mentioned above provide key information for your choreographer. Communicate this in great detail; it will save you a lot of time, stress, and headache on your wedding day while performing your First Dance.

Groom's Attire

Dear Groom, your tuxedo (or your custom made suit) is pretty safe to dance your Wedding Dance in and I have only three small details that you should be aware of before your big day on the dance floor. First, and this is a big little detail, concerns your tuxedo pants! Sometimes, and depending on which of the performance categories you choose, you may be required to squat a little as a preparation for a lift to express something choreographically, or even kneel down on one knee to act out some lyrics from your wedding song. Be 100% sure you can try these movements in your wedding pants before the choreographer puts the routine together to ensure that you're able to squat or kneel down without any incidents, like ripping your pants apart! If you are limited in certain movements, let your instructor know and the routine can be choreographed accordingly, to avoid possible accidents while performing.

The second detail concerns your jacket (tuxedo top). Performing in your suit will make you look strong and very elegant and that, dear grooms, is a fact. Just to be sure, test how high you can raise your arms when you have the jacket on to check if there are any limitations. For example, the shoulders of your jacket and how it's made may or may not allow you to raise your arms higher than slightly above your shoulders. Most of the time, there shouldn't be an issue and you can look forward to turning and twirling your Bride and dancing the night away. Dance in your jacket and wear it during your dance lessons. It is important to practice in your suit to get used to how it feels.

> **Note one:** It is possible to perform your Wedding Dance in your vest, if you think you might be more comfortable. But first, try to dance in your suit, to see which feels

better and communicate with your dance instructor to decide what looks best.

Note two: Gentlemen, I have a choreographic suggestion for you. This can be used in The Surprise Wedding Dance or The Entertainer as a transition from the slow romantic song to the faster entertaining part of your routine. Take your jacket off while dancing, swing it in the air, and throw it into the crowd as part of your act to make a dramatic statement: "The party's starting now!" Your guests will cheer you on, having the best time of their lives. Badass isn't it?!

Attire Accessories

Accessories are a magnificent addition to your wedding attire and they may or may not interfere with your movement during your performance. Generally speaking we have two kinds of accessories: The wedding specific accessories; the ones that can emphasize your neck line (like a beautiful necklace complimenting your wedding dress), the ones giving your clothes beautiful accents (like a scarf around your neck or a veil in your hair), or the ones making the overall look complete (like a hat or a special hairpiece); Then the personal accessories which are part of you, like a neckless that you have been wearing since you were a teenager, a bracelet that means a lot to you or a watch you love the most. These personal details make you, you and without them you may feel naked, at least I do. We look at some of the most common accessories and their impact on your performance. Let's start with the wedding specific accessories first:

- The most common Bride's accessory is a beautiful veil (every little girl's dream). The veil can cause restrictions in movement during figures like turns, dips and lifts, as it gets tangled between the wedding couple.
- Gloves are a noble accessory worn by Brides and Grooms to add elegance and grace to the overall look of the wedding couple. Dancing with gloves may contribute to a

lack of connection between the partners and cause the hands to slip, sometimes even losing the glove during the performance.
- Hats are another great accessory giving the wedding couple a personal touch and a beautiful look. To dance with a hat might be inconvenient in many figures (mostly turns, spins and lifts) and you may lose it while performing. On the other hand, the hat could be incorporated into your choreography and even thrown into the crowd as part of your Wedding Dance.

Let's look at the personal accessories and the impact they may have on your performance. When you practice your Wedding Dance, the personal accessories might not be a problem, but can cause small issues while performing. For example: A favorite bracelet, worn by the Groom or the Bride, can hook on the lace of the wedding dress and interrupt the performance, or even stop the performance for a moment to untangle the bracelet.

Another example: A necklace worn by the Bride can cause issues in figures like dips and lifts. While dancing these figures a necklace can cause minor distractions by getting into your face, or even get tangled in your hair, resulting in awkward moments in your efforts to put it back in place.

There are many other accessories to glamorize your look and give your appearance personalized style. Communicate with your dance instructor to avoid unnecessary incidents with your accessories while performing and decide (either choreographically, or by not wearing them) what would be the best option for your Wedding Dance.

Wedding Music

Live Band versus DJ

The music for your performance is, without a doubt, the most important part of all the points mentioned above. Before you select the song or songs for your First Dance, you need to answer one initial question. Do you have a live band or a DJ to play your wedding song? There are as many pros and cons for a live band as there are for a DJ. Let's take a look.

Live Band

To have a live band playing at your wedding reception has an incredible impact on the atmosphere of your venue. Coming from a competitive dancing background, I definitely prefer to dance to live music, simply because it's magical.

To dance your Wedding Dance to live music comes with challenges though. Live bands often have their own interpretation of songs. In this case, you need to get the band's version of the chosen song in order to choreograph and practice your Wedding Dance. If you decide to perform your Wedding Dance to the original version of the chosen song, the band needs to play the exact version of the original song so your choreography matches precisely. When you dance your First Dance to live music and you have time available for additional practice and rehearsals with the band, I guarantee you, your experience performing to live music will be priceless.

The DJ

DJ's are exceptionally professional. They are able to play the exact version of your selected song or mashup you have created your choreography and practiced your Wedding Dance to. You can rely on this exact version every time. You also have the freedom to put together a play list of your choice (live bands have a limited repertoire) and have your favorite songs playing not just for your Wedding Dance, but the entire wedding reception. Do your research, look up the recommendations, and talk to several DJ's before you make the final decision. Remember, this person will carry the entire event and is responsible for everything from the equipment (microphones, sometimes lights, etc.) to the easy flow of your wedding reception. Take your time and decide wisely.

> **Note:** Make sure your wedding coordinator instructs the DJ about the reception program in detail to guarantee that your event will run smoothly. Before your wedding,

> it is a good idea to give the DJ a list of songs you would like him or her to play at your wedding reception.

Thoughts and Suggestions

If you already booked a live band for your wedding and you can't rehearse with them, there's nothing wrong with dancing your First Dance to a song from a CD or a computer. It will ease the process and decrease the pressure. If you still decide to perform with live, music follow the instruction about the song version in the "Live Band" section and make sure you can practice your Wedding Dance at least a couple of times with the band before your actual performance.

> **Note:** If, for any reason, on the day of your wedding, the band is unable to play your song, have a CD or a flash drive with your wedding song ready as backup. The same thing goes for the DJ. After you communicate and deliver the CD or file with your wedding song, have a backup ready for your wedding day to avoid unnecessary stressful situations.

The Wedding Song(s)

Your wedding song is a big statement. It tells your guests a lot about you as a couple and your relationship. In the process of choosing a song for your performance, you must be aware of a couple of things. First, pay attention to the lyrics. The melody of a song may sound romantic and beautiful, but the lyrics might be about: a heartbreak, one person leaving another, or about being single. Therefore, choose only a song or songs with lyrics that are positive in telling the story about your relationship. In the section "The Lyrics of the Song" we will look at how you can use the lyrics to emphasize some of your movements with the words and create a greater emotional impact on your audience. Another point that will influence your decision about your song selection for your First Dance is the performance category (The Classic, The Entertainer, etc.). The best way to determine which song to choose and how many songs you will need is to communicate with your instructor about the idea for your First Dance and how you want to tell your story. Every performance category already dictates the number of songs needed for your Wedding Dance. Depending on the performance category and how long you want your choreography to be, these songs might need editing (I recommend hiring a professional editor to cut and mix the songs together). But let's take look at different scenarios. The performance category "The Classic," is typically performed to a romantic song of your choice, and in most cases editing won't be necessary. If the song is too long, or the musical highlight is at the end of the song, you might want to cut the middle part out and make it shorter, to have the musical crescendo sooner. It all depends upon the choreography, the desired performance duration, and your preference. The performance categories; The Surprise Wedding Dance, The Entertainer and The Entertainer – Special Edition (sometimes the Themed Wedding Dance) have 2 or more songs included in the performance that need to be cut and arranged in order to create your choreography. You can find some examples of the songs in the section "The Song Examples" on page 84.

Summary

We have covered everything you need to know before you begin to choreograph your Ultimate Wedding Dance. With all the information provided, you now have a clear idea about every aspect of each performance category, and you are definitely closer to knowing and deciding what you want your First Dance to be and to look like. It is important to consider the time factors for each performance, before you decide which performances you'd like to have at your wedding reception. The time needed for dance lessons for all the participants must be anticipated accurately because each performance will require its own schedule.

An Example: Let's say you choose The Entertainer (4-6 weeks and 15-18 dance lessons) as your wedding performance and you'd like to have the Father/Daughter Dance (2-3 weeks and 3-6 dance lessons) and the Mother/Son Dance (2-3 weeks and 3-6 dance lessons) performance. The category "The Entertainer" needs the most time. Therefore, the total time for your preparation will be 4-6 weeks, increasing the number of dance lessons to 18-24 because the preparation for additional performances runs simultaneously with the main category.

Another Example: You choose The Classic (2-3 weeks and 6-9 dance lessons), and you'd like to add the Father/Daughter Dance (2-3 weeks and 3-6 dance lessons) and the Mother/Son Dance (2-3 weeks and 3-6 dance lessons) performance and to have even more fun, the Bride's Solo Dance (2-3 weeks and 6-9 dance lessons). Here, The Classic sets the time needed. The total preparation time will be 2-3 weeks and the total amount of lessons for the Bride is 15-24 dance lessons and the Groom, 12 - 15 Dance lessons. Preparation of any additional performances will run parallel with the main category as well.

Our Checklist

The checklist below provides all the essential components to specify how many performances you'd like to have at your wedding and how much time it takes to put them together. Write down all your information and check off the performances you plan to have in your reception program.

Our Wedding Date _____

_____

Our Wedding Song(s) _____

The Dance Floor (Size) _____

Our Performance Category
- ☐ *The Classic*
- ☐ *The Surprise Wedding Dance*
- ☐ *The Entertainer*
- ☐ *The Entertainer - Special Edition*
- ☐ *The Themed Wedding Dance*

The Layout of the Reception Area

Bride's Attire _____

Groom's Attire _____

Additional Performances
- ☐ *Father/Daughter Dance*
- ☐ *Mother/Son Dance*
- ☐ *Bride's Solo Performance*
- ☐ *Groom's Solo Performance*
- ☐ *Bridesmaids and Groomsmen Solo*
- ☐ *Cutest Members of The Family Solo*

The Budget
- ☐ *6 - 9   Dance Lessons*
- ☐ *9 - 12 Dance Lessons*
- ☐ *12 - 15 Dance Lessons*
- ☐ *15 - 18 Dance Lessons*
- ☐ *18 - 24 Dance Lessons*
- ☐ *_____ Dance Lessons*

Our Venue (Address) _____

_____

Our Notes _____

_____

_____

_____

_____

_____

Chapter 2

The Preparation

The goal of your preparation is to have all the needed information about your event ready (the date of your wedding, the attire, the size of the dance floor and any other useful information) before your first dance lesson and provide them to your instructor to make sure that the choreographing process will run smoothly from the beginning with no unnecessary interruptions. Before we discuss the process of preparation in detail, there are a couple of things you need to consider.

Do We Need Help?

Your First Dance is and should be a special occasion. To dance your Wedding Dance with confidence, be comfortable performing in front of your wedding crowd and enjoy it, you need to ask yourselves a very important question. Do we want to hire professional help? Well, let's think about it. When you plan a wedding, there are so many things to take care of, and hiring a wedding coordinator to take the weight off your shoulders is undoubtedly an excellent idea, isn't it? That's why it shouldn't be any different with your Wedding Dance. I strongly recommend working with a professional choreographer to ensure that your First Dance will not only be original, but most of all, personal (more about this topic in the section "The Choreography" on page 35).

There are thousands of dance instructors and choreographers all over the world ready to help you with your Wedding Dance and you are just a few clicks away from finding one online. Choosing the right choreographer is crucial and in your search, it is necessary to ask a vital question. "Does the instructor have any experience with choreographing wedding dances, and if possible, can he or she provide some references or videos?" To have a professional choreographer on your side is a big plus and you will have one less project on your checklist to think about. If you decide to create your Wedding Dance on your own, I will explain the process and provide specific details for you to understand, and suggest which steps should be done first in order to create the most memorable performance.

Inspiration and Ideas

Once you've answered all the questions and collected information from all the points in the first chapter, the next step in this creative process is to find inspiration for your choreography. Watch some videos on YouTube (in case you haven't done so already) to find out what you like, what looks good and try to dance some of the moves to figure out how it feels. You will be spending time practicing and dancing your routine repeatedly and the fact that it feels good and you like it is important. Save the videos of your favorite moves and show them to your instructor on your first dance lesson and communicate that you'd like to integrate these elements into your wedding performance. This will also help to simplify the choreographing process and save you some time for practice and perfecting your First Dance. Don't forget that the time factor in this process is vital. The more time you have, the easier it will be to learn, memorize, and practice your Wedding Dance, and by doing so, build your confidence to perform in front of the wedding crowd.

Attire Check

The next part of your preparation is your attire and shoe check. I strongly recommend trying your dress/tuxedo on before your first dance lesson to make sure you have no limitations in movement (more about the movement limitations is in the section "Your Wedding Attire" on page 14). If you have some movement limitations, let your dance instructor know to ensure that your dance routine will be adjusted accordingly. Another important part of the attire check are your shoes. I advise you to bring your shoes to every dance lesson and practice session to get used to them. This is a great opportunity to get comfortable not only wearing your shoes, but by wearing them while dancing and breaking them in, you will avoid discomfort or even worse, blisters. Remember, you'll spend an entire day in those shoes and I'm 100% sure you want to be comfortable and enjoy your wedding to the fullest. Good point, isn't it?

Your Wedding Song(s)

The next part of your preparation is choosing a wedding song(s) for your performance before your first dance lesson. Decide with your fiancé which song(s) will express your love for each other the most. Depending on the performance category, you may choose one or more songs for your Wedding Dance, and remember, those songs may need some editing. Once decided, download the song(s) to your playlist (on your smartphone) and make sure you have the right version of the song(s) you would like to use for your choreography. Many songs have different versions and covers and you need to be certain which version you will use. Bring your music to your first dance lesson to start the choreographing process right away. If you have several favorites and you can't decide which one to use, ask your dance instructor which of your songs might be better suited for your wedding performance.

Schedule Changes

This information is crucial for your preparation not only for your choreographer, but it directly affects your performance. It basically dictates the beginning of your dance routine. Before your first dance lesson, communicate with your wedding planner and find out what the schedule of your reception looks like and when will you perform your First Dance.

An example: Let's say your Wedding Dance is scheduled after the toast, and the starting point of your choreography is at the sweetheart table. A day or two before your wedding, you receive an e-mail from your wedding planner about some minor changes in the schedule, not a big deal really (the note says). But instead of dancing your Wedding Dance after the toast (where your starting point is at the sweetheart table), the schedule changed and your Wedding Dance will be performed after the grand entrance and you will be already on the dance floor. You have spent a lot of time and worked very hard on your choreography and more importantly, you are comfortable and confident with your dance performance. Now, since the schedule has changed, the beautiful intro rehearsed so many times cannot be used. The hardest part is that you need to come up with an alternative beginning from the grand entrance (instead of the beginning from the sweetheart table) in less than one or two days, which isn't enough time, therefore changes should be avoided.

Another example: Imagine a similar situation as described in the first example. But, instead of a last minute change in the schedule, the place (your sweetheart table) you are starting your Wedding Dance from has changed. For some reason, your mom thought that you need to be on the stage when doing the toast, so the wedding crowd can see you better. This is indeed a great idea and well-intentioned, but not for you and your Wedding Dance. With this little adjustment, you need to come up with an alternative beginning for your wedding routine in no time. My advice is to avoid changes at the last minute; even trained athletes and professional dancers don't like them.

<u>The Bottom Line is, Avoid Changes at all Cost!</u>

Summary

Your preparation will make the journey towards your Wedding Dance more enjoyable. This includes the decision wheter to hire a professional choreographer or creating a personal Wedding Dance on your own. Having all the information before the first dance lesson will ensure a smooth choreographing process with no interruptions or hang-ups. Based on your ideas and in consideration of the event schedule, your chosen wedding song(s) and your wedding attire, you or your choreographer will have the fundamentals to choose the right performance category and create a wedding dance of your dreams.

The Last Minute Recommendations

If you are reading this part of the book after you have finished reading the section, "The Timeline," I understand you are in a big hurry.

With no further explanation, let's take a look at several things you need to do:

1. Read this book. It will take less than a couple of hours and it will provide you with all the important information you need to know about your Wedding Dance.

2. Choose your wedding song if you haven't done so already.

3. Figure out how much time you have available, a couple of days or weeks perhaps? This is essential information for the next point.

4. Find and contact a choreographer nearby as soon as possible and explain your situation to avoid unnecessary delays.

5. Set up your first dance lesson, or if possible several lessons with your instructor to start the choreographing process immediately.

6. Before your first lesson, check your attire as described in the section, "Your Wedding Attire," on page 14.

7. Don't forget to bring the shoes you intend to perform in, to your dance lessons.

8. After your dance lessons, practice several times a day to make sure you create a muscle memory for your choreography.

9. Dance your wedding routine at least once in front of your close friends to get familiar with the "performing aspect" of your Wedding Dance. It is important to experience how it feels to dance in front of people.

If you are nervous about your performance, the most important thing you should think about is this: The main reason that your family, friends, and guests are coming to your wedding to celebrate your bond and the expression of your love (your Wedding Dance), is You! The only thing you should focus on is the joy of this wonderful occasion.

Our Preparation Checklist

Write your notes in the checklist below; it includes all the important information you need before you put the choreography together. This will help you make the creative process easier.

Dance Instructor _____

Inspirations and Ideas _____
(notes, video files, photo files)

_____
_____
_____
_____
_____
_____
_____
_____
_____
_____
_____
_____

Bride's Attire ☐ _____

Bride's Shoes ☐ _____

Groom's Attire ☐ _____

Groom's Shoes ☐ _____

Wedding Song(s) ☐ _____

_____

_____

_____

Schedule of the First Dance _____

_____

_____

_____

Our Notes

Chapter 3

Choreography

*F*inally, the part you were waiting for the entire time while reading this book, "The Choreography." In this section, we look closely at the process of choreographing and creating a dance routine to the music of your choice. We will also look at the helpful tips and tricks regarding how to tell your story with a dance and explore examples of dance moves and positions that will make you look phenomenal. Are you ready? Let's do this!

The Beginning of your Choreography

As we already discussed in the section, "The Schedule of the Event", the beginning of your choreography will depend on the starting point (where you are in the ballroom) and the schedule prior to your performance (the grand entrance, a speech, or a toast). If your Wedding Dance follows one of those scheduled events, your beginning won't need extra preparation because the start of your performance will connect seamlessly with them. Let's take a look at some examples of how you can start your choreography.

The Beginning from the Grand Entrance

In this example, your Wedding Dance starts after the grand entrance; well, it overlaps with it. The grand entrance has a musical background and the bridal party is introduced while the music is playing. Starting with your Bridesmaids and Groomsmen, followed

The Ultimate Wedding Dance

by the Best Man with the Maid of Honor, and finally you, the wedding couple. If the Wedding Dance follows the grand entrance, the introduction of the wedding couple and their First Dance must be announced together. Otherwise there will be a dull moment between your grand entrance and the actual beginning of your performance, and the natural flow of the event will be interrupted.

The DJ or the MC might say something like this: "Dear guests, I present to you the Bridal Party. Ladies and Gentlemen the Groomsmen and the Bridesmaids; Mr. Travis and Miss Tang, Mr. and Mrs. Lucas, Mr. Long and Mrs. Torres. Dear guests, the Best Man and the Maid of Honor Mr. Stone and Miss Henley. And finally, let's give a hand to the celebrated couple of today, Mr. and Mrs. Banner and their First Dance." The background music will smoothly transition into your wedding song exactly when you arrive at the starting point of your dance routine (usually a couple of feet before the dance floor). I recommend communicating with the DJ or MC where exactly your starting point is beforehand, and rehearse it several times at the main rehearsal. Here are couple of options demonstrating what the beginning of your choreography might look like, after the grand entrance.

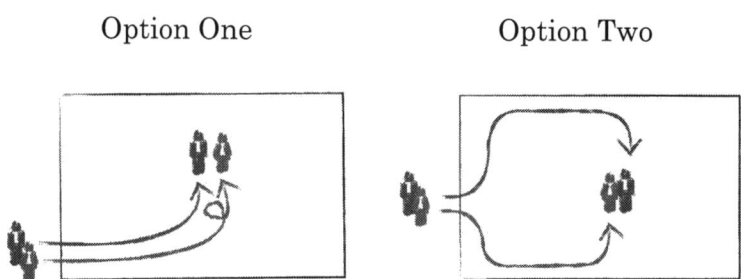

These examples show two possible beginnings for your Wedding Dance and the dance directions, following the grand entrance.

The Beginning from the Sweetheart Table

As you already assumed from the title of this section, your choreography will start at your sweetheart table (usually after a toast or a speech). The announcement may sound like this: "Dear guests, allow me to present Mr. and Mrs. Banner and their First Dance." The start of your routine will depend on your wedding song, its intro, and sometimes the lyrics of the song. If your chosen song has a short intro (2 or 4 bars), you may start you routine with the first lyrics. If a long intro occurs (between 4 and 16 bars) and depending on your choreography, you can advise your DJ or MC to start the music (intro playing in the background) while introducing your First Dance, so you can begin your dance routine with the first lyrics. Make sure your DJ or MC will rehearse the introduction with the music to assure a smooth start. Let's look at some options for the beginning of your choreography from the sweetheart table.

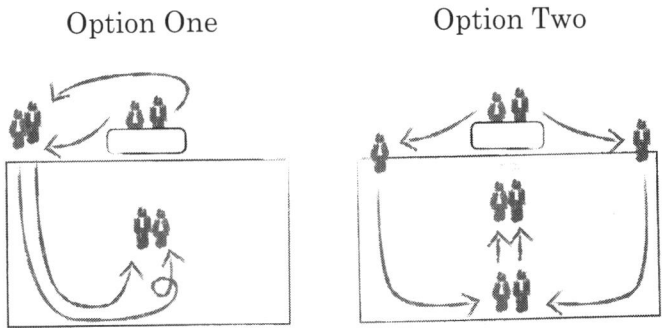

These examples show the position of the sweetheart table in relation to the dance floor and two possible beginnings of your choreography, as well as the dance directions.

A Special Beginning

In this section, we will discuss alternative beginnings of your routine that are out of the ordinary and give your Wedding Dance a different look (choreographically speaking), a personal touch if you will. There are many creative ways to make the beginning of your choreography more entertaining. Be aware that if you choose a special beginning for your Wedding Dance, you will need extra time right before your performance to get to your starting point.

The major factor in this type of beginning is the connection between the scheduled event before your First Dance (the grand entrance, a speech, or a toast) and your actual performance. To assure a smooth transition with no awkward pauses, clearly communicate with your wedding planner and the DJ or MC where in the ballroom or the dance floor you will begin your Wedding Dance, and also how much time you will need to get to the starting point. It is necessary to rehearse the exact timing with your DJ, MC and/or the band at the main rehearsal, to ensure that the transition is effortless and all the participants are on the same page.

Here are a couple of examples of the alternative beginnings of your Wedding Dance.

Example One   Example Two

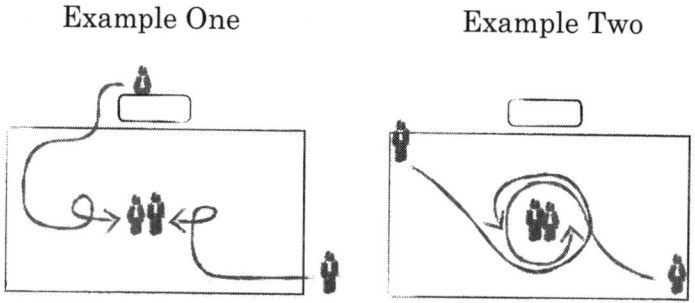

These examples show the position of the sweetheart table in relation to the dance floor, two possible starting points for the special beginning of your Wedding Dance, and the dance directions.

In the first example, the Wedding Dance follows the grand entrance, and as previously discussed in the section "The Beginning from the Grand Entrance", the introduction of the wedding couple and their First Dance should be announced together, but Not in this case! The Groom will escort the Bride to the sweetheart table as part of the grand entrance (the Groom pulls the chair out and helps the Bride sit down gracefully). This is a cue for the DJ or MC to start the announcement of the Wedding Dance, and while doing so, the Groom walks to his starting point where his part of the Wedding Dance begins. Remember, timing is everything! When the Groom arrives at the starting point, the announcement will be done and the wedding song starts to play immediately without a pause. It is important here to make a smooth transition and avoid any dull moments.

The Wedding Dance in the second example shown above will take place after a speech or a toast when the wedding couple is seated at the sweetheart table. The starting point of your performance in this version will be on the dance floor where the couple will face each other, standing at opposite sides of the dance floor. The setup for your Wedding Dance will be very similar to the first example except in this case, the couple will walk onto the dance floor at opposite ends while the DJ or MC is introducing the First Dance of the evening. And guess what? You've got it right! Timing is everything. Make sure the arrival at the starting point and the beginning of your routine is timed exactly with the music and without a pause. I recommend having a few practices beforehand at your main rehearsal so everyone involved understands the timing.

Music Structure

Before we get into the manner of choreographing your Wedding Dance and how to have the most impressive performance, we need to talk about the technical components of your music.

The first and most important one is the signature of the song (timing), in other words, the character of the dance. It can be a classical waltz in 3/4 time signature, or a beautiful, romantic song that is written in 4/4 time signature, also called "common time." Most modern songs today are written this way.

The second and very similar to the signature of a song, is the melody of the song. The melody of a song is usually on top of the time signature and expressed through singing or played by an instrument.

The third, and very powerful tool in creating a memorable choreography, are the lyrics. The best way to create an appealing Wedding Dance is to combine all three components to create a choreography rich in movement that resonates with all the elements of the song. Let's take a closer look.

The Signature of the Song

As already mentioned, the timing of your chosen song dictates the character of the dance. For example, if a song is written in 3/4 time, it means that this song is most likely a Waltz, a Viennese Waltz or an Argentine Vals. The waltz music is counted in sets of threes counting 1, 2, 3, 2, 2, 3 and so on up to 8, 2, 3 and then back to one. This type of dance has very specific figures and if you don't work with a dance instructor, the best way to find out what kind of dance moves are available to you is to go online. There are hundreds of videos of dance steps and figures that you can study and use for your Wedding Dance. The waltz is an upscale, romantic and delightful way to charm your wedding crowd with your elegance and gracefulness.

The 4/4 signature, also called "common time," is a simple structure that many songs use as a base. The timing will start with count 1 and end with count 8 and back to one. As long as you can count to 8, you are good to go. Let's practice for a minute. Ready? And " 1, 2, 3, 4, 5, 6, 7, 8, 1, 2, 3, 4, 5, 6, 7, 8", see: super easy! You can dance your steps on every count, every second count, or alternate, depending on the character of the dance and the idea of your choreography. The combination might look something like this: 1 2 (one slow step on two beats), 3 (step), 4 (step), 5 6 (one slow step on two beats), 7 (step), 8 (step). You've got it. To choreograph and create a wedding routine with this timing (4/4 signature) is very easy and the possible combination of steps, moves, and figures are endless.

The Melody of a Song

Sweet, romantic, harmonious, flowing, pleasant, rhythmic, cheerful, repetitious, quick, slow, energetic and exciting are just a few expressions that can describe the melody of a song. The melody in music is a group of notes of various pitches (how high or low a note sounds), which are played one after the other. Together they make a tune in the same way that a group of words makes a sentence. You can put together steps within your choreography that will highlight the melody of the song and this way, create a distinguished look of your Wedding Dance that will leave your audience astonished.

An example: I'm sure you know the song by Whitney Houston "I Will Always Love You" from the movie "The Bodyguard." This wonderful song has an almost consistent beat throughout the whole song (this is the time signature). There are many melodic highlights within this song, but there are two that everyone remembers. The first is made by a saxophone solo and the other is sung by Whitney's amazing voice. Towards the end of the song, she sings so high and so long that it leaves the audience breathless just listening to it. This is the melodic highlight you are looking for. Here is an idea of what you could do choreographically with this melodic highlight: When she sings this part of the song, the Groom lifts the Bride, spins her and increases the speed of the spin gradually while Whitney increases the intensity of her voice and continues till the end of her solo. After that solo, the music slows down and the Groom puts his lady down slowly and kisses her. I guarantee, your family and friends will talk about your Wedding Dance years after the lights go out, and the most important part of this performance will be the unforgettable memories.

The Lyrics of the Song

Lyrics have an enormous impact on us and can portray feelings and evoke emotions in so many mysterious and unexplainable ways. The strategy of using lyrics is an imaginative and clever way to create a very powerful choreography. The clue you are looking for in the lyrics is a word or a sentence that will emphasize some of your dance moves or gestures.

An example: The lyrics might say "When you hold my hand I understand the magic that you do", and the choreographed moves could look like this: You walk next to each other towards the audience and when the words say "When you hold my hand", the Groom takes the hand of the Bride and while the words of the song say "I understand the magic that you do", the Groom twirls his Bride, dips her, and looks her straight in the eyes while doing so. This is just one of hundreds of possibilities choreographically speaking.

Without further explanation, let's look at the chorus of a song I wrote a couple of years ago: "Just You And I."

The lyrics go like this:

And I will hold your hand
When you walk with me
Through the streets of the city, called life

And I will kiss your lips
When you're holding me
As you listen to my beating heart

Cause then you know, I love you

Within these few lines, you have so many opportunities to use the words to your advantage and express the lyrics with matching movements. Let's find some words and lyrics we can use to emphasize the movements within your choreography. The lines "And I will hold your hand," and "When you walk with me" are straightforward and super easy to translate into movements, suggesting that you hold hands and walk, right? Pretty simple. The next sentence, "And I will kiss your lips," is an invitation to kiss each other. The line, "When you're holding me," gives you artistic permission to hug your spouse on the dance floor. Isn't that great? And the lyric "As you listen to my beating heart" is your cue ladies: you know what to do, but be careful not to press too hard on your man's chest because he has a white shirt on and the makeup will stay there for the whole evening (it is a good idea for the Groom to have an extra shirt ready).

As you see, the lyrics of a song can emphasize your movements enormously and give your performance a special touch. The reason for this is that our brain combines the sight and sound together and the impact of both is much greater than if it's just seen or heard separately.

Note: Be careful when choreographing your Wedding Dance with lyrics. Choose only a few words or sentences (maximum 2-3), to emphasize your dance moves and gestures. Why? Imagine the Las Vegas strip: so many lights, so much going on, and you don't know where to look or go first. It becomes too overwhelming! What you are looking for is an impactful Wedding Dance that inspires your audience not only choreographically, but also emotionally without over-choreographing your routine.

Basic Positions and Dance Moves

This section is dedicated to the extremely useful and specific positions that you can find in every Wedding Dance. It will provide you with some dance material for your wedding routine. We will also take a glimpse at some of the dance moves that you can use throughout your choreography.

The Basic Position

Let's start with the most recognizable dance position that the dance community has known for centuries: the basic position. When you attend a formal event where you can also dance, you use this position to dance every time. The couple is facing each other, the gentleman puts his right hand on the lady's shoulder blade or around her waist, and the lady puts her left hand on top of his right shoulder. The gentleman's left hand and lady's right hand meet in the middle, approximately at the height of woman's shoulder, the same way you would greet someone with a high five (palms facing each other). Then, both partners turn their hands counterclockwise and close their fingers around each other's hands. This position is very simple, noble looking, and can be used in your choreography as a connection between the other dance moves throughout your Wedding Dance as needed.

The Prom Dance Position

The second position is the same position you might have used to dance at your high school prom. The gentleman places his hands on the lady's waist above the hips and the lady puts her arms on top of his shoulders. So many memories.

The Double Hand Hold Position

You might remember the scene from the movie "Titanic," when Jack and Rose escaped below the deck (as Jack referred to "the real party") and the moment on the stage where they spun holding hands and danced the night away. This position is simple and good looking, used mostly as a connection between movements. The wedding couple is facing each other and holding both hands.

The Underarm Turn

The underarm turn can be danced from several dance positions and is one of the basic figures no wedding choreography should miss. Let's take a look at the combination from the basic position. To turn the Bride from this position, the Groom lifts his left hand to lead the Bride and give her a signal for the turn. Simultaneously this creates a space for the Bride to turn under the Groom's arm (the direction of Bride's turn will be to her right). After the turn, the couple may come back to the basic position or any other position that can be danced after the

turn, like the side by side position (see page 78), or the double hand hold position.

The Walk-Around and Slow Underarm Turn

The next two dance moves explained in this section will create a beautiful and rich movement on the dance floor. Those figures can be danced from several dance positions. For easier visualization and better understanding, we will look at an example from the side by side position which can be used at any point of your choreography.

Let's start with the Walk-Around figure. Initially, the couple is standing side by side, holding hands, and facing the same direction (approximately 3-4 feet from each other and the Bride is on Groom's right side). The Groom stands still and leads the Bride around him in a circle. At the point when the Groom's right arm is across his body (the Bride walks approximately half a circle), the Groom lifts his arm above his head so the Bride can continue to walk around him and complete the whole circle. This particular figure can also be done from the opposite side. Here, the Bride's position is on the Groom's left side and the Groom leads his lady with his left arm.

The beginning of the slow underarm turn from the side by side position is the same as the walk-around figure, except the Groom will walk against the Bride's direction. When the couple arrives at the point where they cross paths, the Groom lifts his arm to allow the Bride to walk under his arm to complete the slow underarm turn. This elegant dance move can be done from either side and can be used throughout your dance routine, depending on the choreography.

You will find a detailed photographic guide for the walk-around figure and the slow underarm turn in the section "The Visual Examples of Dance Positions and Figures" on page 78.

Dips and Lifts

Incorporating dips and lifts into your Wedding Dance is a wonderful way to make your choreography look more interesting. It will give your routine the special something and a personal touch that your wedding crowd will surely appreciate. Like the cute wedding couple on top of your wedding cake, dips and lifts are a beautiful detail complimenting the overall look of your performance.

Dips

Remember the great romantic movies that left a big impression on us and how we perceive romance? A final scene where the male lead dips the leading female into a pose, and as she lays in his arms, he's telling her, "You are the love of my life," and then kisses her passionately till the screen fades? A simple dip in your wedding choreography can give your wedding guests an unforgettable and emotional experience that will leave them speechless. You will find more examples of dips in the section, "Visual Examples of Dance Positions and Figures," on page 78.

Lifts

Lifts in your choreography are another useful way to create an extraordinary and spectacular Wedding Dance that will make your audience stand up and cheer. Such wedding performances will create long lasting memories for the rest of your lives, not to mention the countless views and likes on social media.

The Classic Lift

We have all seen movies that melt our hearts and shape our expectations about romantic gestures and behaviors in our lives. The first lift of its kind, associated with a wedding, is a lift used by the Groom to carry the Bride through the doorstep of their home after the wedding. It is also used in some cultures to carry the Bride into the ballroom after the wedding ceremony. How does this lift work? To lift the Bride, the Groom puts his right arm around the Bride's waist and with his left arm, he takes her  legs while she hugs him around the neck. To put the Bride down, the Groom lets her legs go first, while holding her tightly around the waist till she stands safely on the ground. This beautiful and simple lift can also be done along with one or several spins at any point in your Wedding Dance, depending on the choreography.

The Basic Face to Face Lift

This is a romantic and very intimate lift that you can implement throughout your entire choreography, or as a highlight of your Wedding Dance (think of the kissing scene in the rain from the movie, "The Notebook"). It goes like this: The couple is facing each other and standing very close together as you would dance at your prom. The Groom slightly bends his knees as a preparation for the lift and puts both arms around the Bride's waist, making sure he is holding her tight. Then he lifts her  up while the Bride's arms are around the Groom's neck. To bring the Bride back to the floor, the Groom bends his knees once again to let her down safely. In addition, while the Bride gracefully glides in the air, the couple can kiss and/or spin a couple of times to make this lift more interesting. The choreographic choice and the styling of this lift depends on the music and the actual routine.

The Extended Face to Face Lift

Dear Grooms, if you feel strong and you want to take this lift to the next level, I have a "cool" upgrade for you. The lift, and how it works, will be the same except in the preparation. You will bend your knees more (like a half of a squat - don't forget to check on your pants) and put your arms around the Bride's thighs (instead of her waist), and lift her from there. The Bride's elbows, in this case, need be on top of your shoulders to support herself and help you with this lift. This way, you can lift the Bride much higher and create a different look. You can  add a spin to this type of lift as well, but be careful, it might get both of you a little dizzy. To bring the Bride back down, you will bend your knees once again and lower your Bride gently back to the dance floor. This stylish version of the lift can be used at any point during your choreography or for the ending of your Wedding Dance.

The Spinning Face to Face Lift

For those couples who want to make this lift even more interesting and take things to a totally different level, there is an exciting option for you, which is used strictly for the ending of your Wedding Dance. I'll explain why. This lift is challenging, but I guarantee, your wedding crowd will be stunned and hold their breaths until the Bride is safely back on the dance floor. Are you curious? Let's look at how this lift is done. It starts exactly the

same way as the basic version of this lift with a spin. The Groom's arms will be around the Bride's waist. The Bride's arms, and this is the most important part of this lift, must be around the Groom's neck very tightly while grabbing each elbow with her hands to have a secure grip, but be careful not to choke your Groom, ladies. The Groom lifts the Bride up and spins her till he reaches a speed where the Bride's legs swing up into the air due to the momentum. You can spin in either direction, depending on which feels more comfortable for you. When the momentum is established, the Groom lets go of the Bride's waist and opens his arms to create a breathtaking scene. To bring the Bride back down to the dance floor, the Groom must decrease the speed of the spin and put his arms back around the Bride's waist till she is safely back on the floor. This is a remarkable way to glamorize the ending of your Wedding Dance.

> **Performance Note:** This type of movement can make you very dizzy. To avoid dizziness after this figure is complete, stay in closed position for a few seconds to regain stability. In case you lose balance and you find yourself laying down on the dance floor at the end of your performance, make it seem it is a part of your extravagant ending.

The Deer Jump Lift

This is a phenomenal looking lift with a funny name that can be a marvelous addition to your wedding performance. This type of lift uses momentum to make the figure look easier and more interesting. Therefore, it is necessary for the Groom to move while lifting the Bride. You can choose one of three movements to execute this lift; walking in a straight line, spinning, or a combination of the two, called pivoting. Let's take a look at this spectacular lift in detail and how it's done. The Bride will stand with her left side very close the Groom's right side creating a reverse L shape with their bodies, looking from above, like so _| and touching their hips and chest. The Bride's left arm will be around the Groom's neck (the Bride's armpit needs to be on top of the Groom's shoulder to help him with the lift). The Groom puts his right arm very tightly around the Bride's waist and bends his knees in preparation for lifting the Bride from the floor. To make this lift easier, the Groom can push his hips forward while lifting the Bride and lean slightly back with his upper body. To bring the Bride back to the floor, the Groom bends his knees gradually to assure a smooth and graceful transition (air to ground). Before we go into detail of each version of this lift, let me explain why it is called "The Deer Jump Lift". While in the air, the Bride elevates her legs into a half split as if she would jump. The position of her legs, one leg bent and the other leg straight, creates a silhouette of a deer jumping. The position of the Bride's legs can vary depending on the styling and the choreography.

> **Note:** This lift can be done from either side depending on the choreography and your preference (some Grooms might be more comfortable lifting the Bride from the right side and some from the left).

> **Note for the Bride:** Your front leg must be the one closer to the Groom. For example: If the Groom lifts you with his right arm, you will be standing on his right side with your left side, and while being lifted, your left leg will be stretched to the front.

CHOREOGRAPHY

The Walking Version of the Deer Jump Lift

As already mentioned, momentum is used to make this lift easier and smoother. This lift can be executed from a stationary position (when the Bride and Groom are standing together), while moving (the couple is moving in the same direction) or when the Bride is moving towards the Groom. Depending on your choreography, you can use any of these options to start the lift. For example: In your dance routine, you walk apart and when the music crescendo starts, the Bride runs towards the Groom passing by very closely in front of him. At this point, the Groom puts his arm around the Bride's waist, lifts her off the floor and walks in a straight line while creating a floating motion for the viewers. The duration of the lift is determined by the music and your choreography. This type of lift is suited mostly for the middle part of your choreography and it is a wonderful element, an appetizer if you will, to build up the excitement for the grand finale of your Wedding Dance.

The Turning Version of the Deer Jump Lift

This version of the lift is a sensational highlight that can finish your Wedding Dance with a spectacular statement. This lift can also be used throughout your dance routine. You can start this lift from a stationary position or while moving, but to begin from a movement is more challenging. The preparation is the same as described earlier. When you begin this lift from a stationary position, it is necessary that you start the spin right away and use the momentum of the spin to make lifting easier. If you enter into this lift while moving (either when the Bride moves towards the Groom or both walk in the same direction), the Groom must take a few steps after he lifts the Bride to establish a good position and a secure grip. If the Groom begins the spin right away, the momentum will pull the Bride away from his body and make the figure unbalanced and uncomfortable for both of them.

Note: If you have difficulties doing this lift with one arm, you can help yourself with the other arm if needed. While lifting, the Groom holds his free arm close to his body in front of him (the palm of his hand is facing up) and the Bride's free arm connects with his hand (the Bride's arm is straight in front of her body pushing against the Groom's hand). This way the lift becomes manageable and easier to do.

Summary

The choreographing process is rather complex, but totally doable. The most important topic and the beginning of this creative process is your story. The next step is the overall look of your choreography (the image) and how you want to express your story. This is where the performance categories come into play. What do you want your Wedding Dance to look like? Do you want it to be a romantic Cinderella fairytale? Then you should definitely choose "The Classic" for your Wedding Dance. If you want your Wedding Dance to be more wild, "The Entertainer" is just the right performance for you. I'm sure you've got the idea.

To put your routine together, you need to consider the starting point of your Wedding Dance. The beginning of your First Dance depends on the placement of your performance in the schedule of the day, the chosen song (slow, fast or a medley), and the style of your performance (The Classic, The Surprise Wedding Dance, etc.). Once you have all the components assembled, the choreographing process can begin. The simplest way to put your routine together is to write down a list of your ideas: what dance moves you would like in your routine, which lifts and positions you would like to incorporate into your Wedding Dance, and whether you would like to use some props in your choreography to make your Wedding Dance unique. You can use your own sources of inspiration as well as the examples in this book.

With this list of ideas, and also some videos, half of the work will already be done. Then, the only thing left, is to put all those elements together: the beginning (according to your performance category and the intro of your wedding song), the middle part (in consideration of the melody and the lyrics), and the spectacular ending matching the musical highlight of your wedding song. This will make your dance not only interesting, but also personal and ultimately your own. And don't forget: Have fun with it!

What's next

Find a choreographer nearby for your convenience, that suits you the best and transforms your ideas into the Wedding Dance of your dreams. For those of you who are more ambitious, follow the plan elements in the chapter "The Choreography" and create a wedding performance matching your unique personalities.

Our Choreography Checklist

I've created, your own personal checklist for you that will help you as a guideline with the choreographing process whether you work with a professional choreographer to help you with your Wedding Dance or, take this journey on your own.

The Beginning of your Wedding Dance ☐ *After the Grand Entrance*
☐ *From the Sweetheart Table*
☐ *A Special Beginning*

Signature of your Wedding Song(s) _____

_____

Melody of your Wedding Song(s) _____

_____

Lyrics of your Wedding Song(s) _____

_____

_____

_____

_____

_____

_____

Positions and Dance Moves _____

_____
_____
_____
_____

Lifts and Dips _____

_____
_____
_____
_____

Our Notes

chapter 4

Practice

*P*ractice is an awesome way to gain confidence, not only in your dancing, but especially in your performance skills. Your practice time will determine how comfortable you will be with your Wedding Dance, as well as how you will feel performing in front of your guests. The goal of your practice is not to think about your steps and figures, but the smoothness of your movements while performing your Wedding Dance.

Helpful Tools

We live in the world of technology. It is a part of our everyday life and it has an incredible impact on everything around us. The smartphones of today can take pictures and videos of high quality and do other incredible things.

To simplify the learning process, video the parts of your routine after every lesson to make sure you won't forget any steps. Have the videos ready every time you practice your Wedding Dance. I recommend creating a separate folder in your phone for your Wedding Dance routine. After the choreography is done, record the whole routine with the music and make sure it is exactly the way you want the final performance to look. You will use this video not only for your practice, but also to watch it on the day of your wedding to review the choreography and give yourself a boost of confidence right before your "big performance." This video will be also very useful in explaining to your videographer what your Wedding Dance looks like to assure that the angles and the lighting are set up correctly to achieve the best quality of the recording. It will also give the videographer an idea of how you move throughout your choreography and where on the floor you will be, so he or she isn't in your way while you are performing. Often, the newlyweds hire two or more videographers and a photographer, and they should definitely know beforehand what your First Dance looks like.

Memorizing of your Choreography

There are lots of techniques that can teach you how to memorize a dance routine, but the most effective technique of all is repetition. Imagine a guitar player practicing chords or playing a song repeatedly to the point where he or she can do it blindfolded without thinking about it. Repetition will help you memorize your routine and take the pressure off, so you can focus on the performance aspect of your Wedding Dance. This is the fun part of performing.

> **Note:** To dance your wedding routine repeatedly may become boring, but the rewards are priceless. In stressful situations, like dancing in front of a crowd, you may forget parts of your choreography, but don't worry. When you have memorized your routine with many repetitions, regardless of how nervous you might be, your muscle memory will save your wedding performance.

Helpful Suggestions

A very helpful addition to your practice is listening to the final version of your wedding song or the final cut of your medley of songs. After your routine is choreographed (or the first parts of it) listen to your wedding song and visualize your dance routine in your mind. This will contribute to the memorizing process. Another helpful tool when performing a dance routine to a specific song is to let the music guide you through your choreography.

You have several options how to do that: The count (1, 2, 3, 4, etc.), the melody (the melodic changes high and low), and the lyrics (certain lyrics of the song that you can associate with your movements). The count is a basic way to learn your dance routine and is very straight forward. The melodic changes can contribute to the memorizing of some parts of your choreography, especially the changes from one movement to another. After a while, as you practice your dance routine, it will be quite easy for you to hear these changes. The lyrics of your wedding song are probably the most helpful tool for memorizing your entire Wedding Dance. If you have lyrics that emphasize some of your movements (as mentioned in the section "The Lyrics of the Song" on page 41) there will be no problem in remembering those particular segments. This, on the other hand, is a strategy for memorizing your choreography with the help of the lyrics. Let me give you an example on how you can use notes to memorize your dance routine more efficiently.

Here are the lyrics:

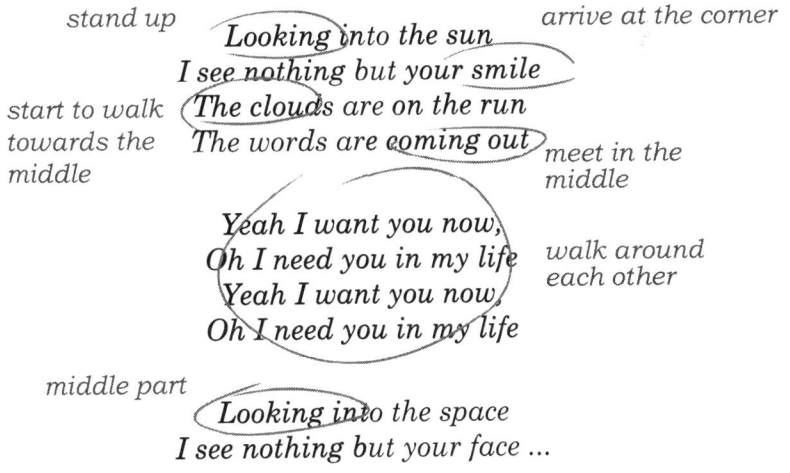

Let's visualize that the starting point of the Wedding Dance is at the sweetheart table. The song starts with an intro of 16 counts (the couple is seated while the intro is playing), and then the first lyrics are sung: "Looking into the sun." While the intro is playing, the introduction of the Wedding Dance will be announced so that the couple can begin their performance with the first lyric. Then, with the lyrics of the first and second sentence, the Groom will walk to the left and the Bride to the right corner of the dance floor. The second part of the routine will start with the words: "The clouds are on the run," and each partner walks around the floor until they meet in the middle. The beginning of the next part of the choreography can be memorized with the words: "Yeah I want you now, Oh I need you in my life ..." which is the part when the newlyweds walk around each other. After that, when the lyrics goes, "Looking into the space," the next part of your routine begins.

Here is a visual example:

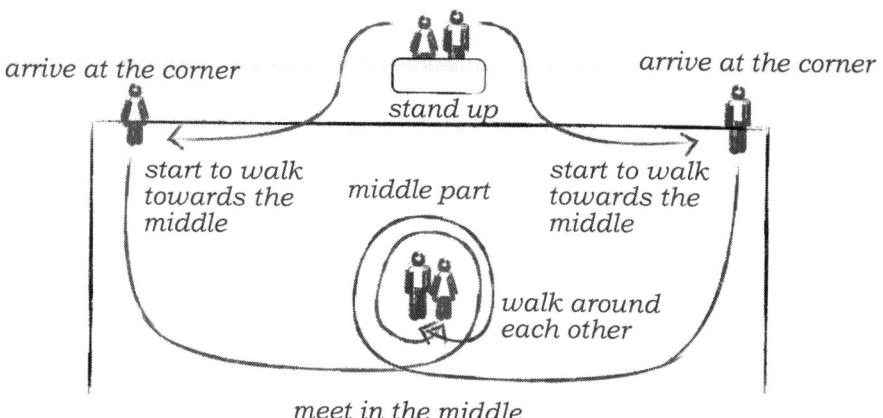

meet in the middle

To make the memorizing process even easier, print out the lyrics of your wedding song, and write your notes (the figures and the moves of your choreography) directly on this paper next to the lyrics. For every new section of your wedding choreography, make a written note to memorize your routine, which creates an easy to understand guideline for what comes next. This simple technique has helped many of the wedding couples I've worked with and simplified the memorizing process.

Practice with your Shoes and Attire

An important part of your preparation should also be to practice with your actual wedding clothes and the shoes you will wear on your "big day" (remember, this will break in your shoes and prevent any blisters). As mentioned in the section "Your Wedding Attire" on page 14, your preparation will eliminate all the possible issues causing concerns and stress before or while you are performing your Wedding Dance.

Dear Brides, I understand that you don't want your fiancé to see you in your gorgeous wedding dress before the wedding, so how can you practice in it? I suggest you find a similar dress with the same volume of the skirt as your wedding dress. Another option is to use the petticoat or underskirt to imitate the volume of your dress. You need to experience how it feels to dance in a skirt or dress like that and your Groom needs to experience dancing with you while you are wearing it.

Time Management

Living in a world where everything is happening at the speed of light, it is very challenging to find a moment to relax, or even find time for projects other than your daily routine. To make your practice more productive, I will suggest step by step instructions to manage your time more efficiently and effectively. The first thing you need to do is decide how much time you are willing to reserve for your dance lessons and your practice. Your dance lessons will be dedicated to choreographing and learning your dance routine and the practice time to perfecting it. An example: Let's say, you chose "The Entertainer" for your Wedding Dance which requires between 4-6 weeks or 15-18 dance lessons prior to your wedding date. Approximately 9-12 lessons (depending on the complexity of your routine) will be needed to choreograph your Wedding Dance and the rest of the lessons to learn it. Besides the dance lessons, you should have time for practicing your dance routine with and without music. This time is very important and should be a part of the learning process to make sure that not only your mind remembers the routine, but also your body. This practice strategy will make your performance look effortless (from muscle memory) and stress-free because of your acquired confidence.

The Practice Timetable

Dear engaged couple, I'm sure you're thinking that the commitment to learn and practice your Wedding Dance takes an incredible amount of time. I assure you that 15-20 minutes of your time per practice session is more than enough (besides your dance lessons) to achieve a decent performance level.

When you are putting together a timetable for your practice, the first thing you need to do with your fiancé is to commit to it. Let me quote the great Tony Robbins: "If your Why?! is big enough, you'll definitely make it happen." Your why could be: to perform your Wedding Dance so well that your wedding guests will be speechless after your performance, or you want to have unforgettable memories, or maybe you want to share the joy of your relationship with your guests through your First Dance. Whatever your goal will be, commit to the schedule 100% . Let's take a look at a possible timetable. Your performance category might be "The Entertainer" with 15-18 dance lessons starting 4-6 weeks before your wedding day. To make the equations easier, we can simplify and calculate 16 dance lessons and 4 weeks of preparation. Two lessons twice a week is just the right amount of time to create and finish your wedding routine as well as to perfect it. Imagine you have your lessons Tuesdays and Fridays which leaves you with 5 days a week to practice. The choreographing process will be as follows: The first week (the first 4 lessons), you'll have about one third of your choreography done. Your practice session (15-20 minutes) during the week should be the day right after the day of your lessons (if your lesson is on Tuesday, your practice would be on Wednesday and so on) to maintain the consistency in your learning process. The second week, representing four more lessons, will take you through two thirds of your choreography and the practice time will increase to 3 times within this week (once after each day of lessons and an additional practice session over the weekend).

Then the third week of 4 more lessons will complete your routine (depending on the complexity of your Wedding Dance), and your practice time increases to four times within this week. The fourth week (the last week before your wedding and the last 4 lessons), you will be working on finishing your choreography, practicing, and preparing for your big performance.

> **Note:** Some people might prefer to practice longer, one or two hours at a time, by combining their practice sessions together. From my experience and the experience of many colleagues, I would recommend to practice several days for 15-20 minutes (or longer) at a time because frequent repetition will help your bodies to memorize your choreography easier and also faster. Remember, repetition is the key.

Practice How to Perform

This section is not only about the practice itself, but about the "how to perform" your Wedding Dance. As a ballroom dancer or any dancer that performs on a stage, the "how to perform" in front of an audience is an inevitable and necessary part of their training.

In addition to numerous competitive students, I have worked with countless wedding couples around the world over the last 20 or more years. The one thing they were truly thankful for was the advice I've given every single one of them: "Once your Wedding Dance is choreographed and you can dance it to the music, perform your dance routine in front of friends, parents, or even your neighbors (well, the ones you've invited to the wedding) to experience performing in front of people". Believe it or not, this often overlooked step will give you great confidence and make you more comfortable with performing.

The Rehearsal

After hours of planning, preparation, dedication and assistance of so many people, you come together for a final rehearsal within days before your wedding. Every detail of your entire wedding ceremony will be rehearsed and last-minute notes taken by your wedding coordinator at the venue to ensure that your wedding runs smoothly. Every person involved in your performance (the photographer, camera crew, lighting personnel and the DJ or live band) should already know your wedding choreography, and the rehearsal should focus on blending every aspect of your performance together. When rehearsing your dance routine, make sure the lights and/or spotlights are on, so you can get used to the brightness (lighting can often be a distraction). The goal of your Wedding Dance rehearsal should not only be about your Wedding Dance itself, but also about the moments leading into it and what happens afterwards. This will assure that every person involved knows where to be and what to do while you are performing.

> **Note:** Make sure your wedding coordinator directs the catering personnel and assigns their positions in the venue for the duration of your performance, to ensure that they will not interrupt or compromise your Wedding Dance in any way.

Summary

To make the learning process easier, video all parts of your dance routine after every lesson and when completed, the final version of the choreography. You will use these videos as a tool in your practice along with the printed lyrics (to write your notes) to memorize your Wedding Dance faster and easier. As you learn and practice your choreography frequently, you will develop muscle memory that will assure a smooth and stress-free performance. With every repetition of your Wedding Dance along with the music you will think less about your steps and focus more on the "performance part" of your routine. Don't forget to dance your routine (at least once) in front of few people to experience how it feels to perform for an audience. The main rehearsal should not only be about your Wedding Dance itself, but also the flow of the scheduled events connected with your performance.

Our Practice Checklist

The practice checklist below is a convenient way to guide you through your practice schedule. It will also help you keep track of your dance lessons and how many times you have practiced your dance routine with and without music. It also serves as a space to make practice notes.

Dance Lessons						
	1	2	3	4	5	6
	7	8	9	10	11	12
	13	14	15	16	17	18
	19	20	21	22	23	24

Practice Sessions						
(15-20 minutes)	1	2	3	4	5	6
	7	8	9	10	11	12

Practice with Music						
(your dance routine)	1	2	3	4	5	6
	7	8	9	10	11	12

Performing in front of an Audience	1	2	3	4	5	6

Our Choreography Questions _____

_____

_____

_____

_____

Our Timing Questions

Our Rehearsal Notes

Our Notes

Chapter 5

Other Details

*B*efore we talk about your performance on the day of your wedding and how to prepare for your First Dance, we need to address the seemingly small details that can give your wedding routine the perfect final spark and make your Wedding Dance an unforgettable treat for the eyes.

The Props

Being a part of an opera production, numerous shows, and other stage performances as a dancer and later on as a choreographer, I've learned the magic of using props to create a mesmerizing atmosphere. Props have the power to pull the audience into an amazing world of a story told with an unforgettable performance. There are countless ways of using props to make your Wedding Dance look special and personal! A single prop used in a choreography, can be a very interesting addition to some of the dance performance categories, especially "The Entertainer" and "The Themed Wedding Dance," but "The Classic" and "The Surprise Wedding Dance" are not excluded. It could be a piece of light fabric like chiffon, satin, or silk matching the colors of your wedding, a chair integrated into your choreography or it could be as simple as a beautiful rose. Those additional little details within your dance routine can enrich and elevate your Wedding Dance to another dimension and make your choreography playful, interesting, and more entertaining. Here are a couple of examples of how you can use props to your advantage.

Let's imagine the starting point of your performance is at the sweetheart table, and after the music starts, the Groom stands up and walks over to a table on the opposite side of the dance floor where he picks up a red rose (an assistant can put the rose on the table before your performance) and begins the dance routine from there. The story might go as follows: The Groom finds a beautiful rose that reminds him of the love of his life (the Bride) and he dances with the rose as if it's her. Once he sees his Bride, he makes his way across the dance floor and gives her the rose as a symbol of his love inviting her to dance and win her over with his dance skills.

In the next example, you might use a piece of light fabric (approximately 9x3 feet, imagine a long scarf) for your Wedding Dance. Starting in the middle of the dance floor, lights are off, and the couple have the fabric wrapped around their waists (each partner has half the fabric), standing with their backs to each other. When the romantic waltz music starts, the spotlights go on (more about lighting in the next section), and the Bride and the Groom will slowly unwrap themselves until they stand across from each other, while holding the fabric stretched between them. As the music continues, the couple will swing the delicate fabric high in the air letting it go. While it gracefully falls like a white cloud from the sky the newlyweds walk towards each other and meet in the middle at the same time as the fabric lands on the dance floor by their feet. A dramatic scene such as this, combined with the spotlights, will make the beginning of your wedding performance unique and extraordinary.

Another example could be a sensual performance of an Argentine Tango, and the prop in this case could be a chair in the middle of the dance floor. This out of the ordinary performance requires a special beginning setup (see the section "A Special Beginning" on page 37). In the beginning of the performance, the Groom is sitting on a chair in the middle of the dance floor. Once the music starts, the Bride walks flirtatiously towards the Groom, and as she passes by, he grabs her hand passionately and spins her, then dips her into a dramatic pose (staring at each other and almost kissing). What a great way to start a Wedding Dance, don't you think?

These are just a few of many choreographic examples with a prop that can add a magical spark to your Wedding Dance and elevate your performance.

The Lighting and Spotlights

The help of a single spotlight, or lights in general (if the venue allows it), can be an incredibly useful tool to make your performance look more remarkable. Imagine a stage performance where the lights create an atmosphere that pulls the audience into a world of magic and wonder. Using lighting can make your performance look phenomenal, but using lights in the wrong way can cause a disaster. Let's look at some of the basic rules and setup guidelines.

The first basic rule is the contrast that lights create, and in your case, the contrast between the dance floor and the audience lighting. The dance floor should always be brighter than the audience. The ideal setting is to only have lighting on the dance floor at the time of your performance. This will focus the attention of the guests on the performing couple: You.

The second basic rule concerns the color of the lighting. If you have the option to choose the color(s) of your lights, it is a wonderful feature and a beautiful addition to your wedding. For your wedding performance, I recommend to use only white lights, white spotlights (with a dimming option) or the blackout option. Unless you hire an extremely experienced choreographer who will direct the setup of the lighting with colors or your Wedding Dance is a big production in the range of "The Entertainer" or "The Entertainer - Special Edition," I recommend using only white lighting for your wedding performance.

The third basic rule: The use of spotlights for your Wedding Dance is an extremely powerful tool that creates a romantic and intimate atmosphere for your wedding performance. This dramatic option (if you have this feature) is especially helpful not only to emphasize your performance, but to highlight the important parts of your choreography that have a significant meaning.

The Ultimate Wedding Dance

An example: Imagine the Wedding Dance starting point is at the edge of the dance floor after the grand entrance. Introducing the First Dance and dimming the lights is happening simultaneously. When the music starts, the spotlight will light up and point directly at the newlyweds holding hands and staring into each other's eyes while walking to the middle of the floor. The spotlight follows them and once they arrive at the place where the choreography continues, the dance floor lights brighten and the spotlight goes off. As the choreography advances to the middle part, the lights will dim again and the spotlight will emphasize a romantic pose or an intimate part of the routine. While dancing the final part of the choreography, all the lights will brighten together with the musical climax as the wedding couple performs the spectacular ending of their Wedding Dance.

> **Note One:** If the spotlight is used in combination with the dimming option of the dance floor lighting, the spotlight can stay on for the entire performance. That way, the light coordinator only dims the dance floor lights as needed.

> **Note Two:** The spotlights should always be positioned behind the audience and pointing towards the dance floor, otherwise the audience might be blinded. See the graphic explanation below.

The Ballroom Lighting Contrast   *The Positioning of the Spotlights*

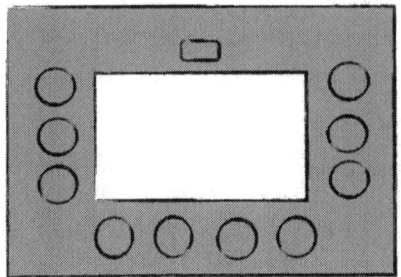 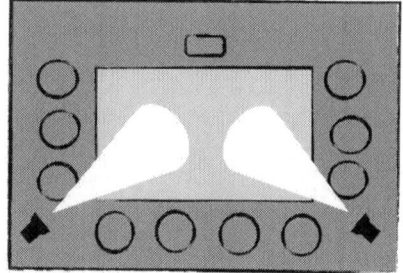

The Photographer and Videographer Crew

To have a great photographer and a videographer (later referred to as "the crew") is as important as a wedding coordinator, DJ, live band, MC, and not to forget, an experienced Wedding Dance choreographer. The photos and the video of your entire wedding (as well as the preparation) will remind you of the moments of your wedding day for life. I'm sure your great grandchildren will watch your wedding video with great curiosity and fascination; the wedding ceremony, the cocktail hour, parents crying with happiness, the silly friend that causes trouble, the heart-melting Best Man's speech, but most of all, the heart and soul of your wedding, your First Dance. In this section, we look at where in the ballroom the crew should be to create the best possible angles to take the ideal pictures and videos.

As already mentioned (in the section "Helpful Tools" on page 57), the first thing to do is to communicate and show the recording of your entire Wedding Dance to the crew. They must know your choreography, the positions, the flow of your dance routine, and where you will be on the dance floor in particular parts of your performance to capture the essence of your Wedding Dance.

> **Note:** To make it easier for you and the crew, your choreographer should record a master shot (wide angle) of your Wedding Dance, and another video, where the camera follows you and captures the details of your choreography (like touching each other's hands, a kiss, or a significant pose).

An experienced photographer as well as a videographer knows how to position a camera to capture the best pictures and videos possible. The shooting direction should be the same as the direction of the spotlights, but beside the audience. The position of the photographer and the videographer in the ballroom while you are performing your Wedding Dance is crucial not only for the final photos and video, but for your performance in general (it is important that the crew does not cross your or each other's path while doing their job).

Another especially challenging aspect of their task is to capture the pictures and the video while your audience is watching your wedding performance. The crew should not obstruct the view of your guests. They need to strategically position themselves in a way that allows your wedding crowd to experience your live performance and enjoy the expression of your love to the fullest, and still complete their task.

Summary

Let's review this section. You are probably wondering why you must know about things like the props, the lighting, the photographer and videographer, especially when you hire these professionals to take care of all these aspects of the wedding themselves. The answer is simple: Awareness! Once you are aware of these things, more likely you won't leave these details to chance. What I have learned over the years (which applies not only to dancing, choreographing, and production of shows) is that when more people focus on the same outcome, there is less room for error.

Your Notes

chapter 6

The Big Day - Your Wedding Performance

The Big Day

The day has come: Your Wedding. Everyone is excited and looking forward to this blissful day, especially your mom who is eager to help, organize and direct everything and everyone, am I right? But all jokes aside, your Wedding Dance is probably the last thing you will be thinking about. This particular section is dedicated to the preparation for your performance and how to remember your choreography during these stressful times. I will give you several suggestions on how to stay calm and what you can do to remember your dance routine. I will also help you to take the stress off your shoulders before and during your big performance to make this experience "one of a kind" but most of all, a pleasant one. But let's start from the very beginning.

The Evening Before

The evening before your wedding may seem busier than your actual wedding day. You will be greeting your family, friends, and your guests at the wedding location or at your home. This beautiful and pleasant pre wedding experience is full of socializing, entertaining of guests. For many wedding couples it is enormous fun, and sometimes exhausting. Well, usually both. After a wonderful evening with your family and friends, you will finally get to your room and have a moment for yourselves to relax (or if the tradition requires, alone without your spouse to be) and enjoy some quiet time to recharge before your "big day." This is one of the many moments when you can go over your choreography and watch the video of your dance routine to review it and, if you are not too tired, even practice it. Just a few minutes of your time and attention will remind your body of the choreography.

The Morning of the Wedding

Regardless of the schedule and the type of wedding, you will have a very busy morning: hair and makeup, getting dressed, people running around, photos are taken, camera crew filming everything, and on top of all this, you might even forget to eat breakfast.

But when you wake up, and before all this madness begins, there is another quiet moment to review your wedding routine right in your bed. Watching the choreography and listening to your wedding song will put you into a wonderful place and allow you to start your wedding day in an uplifted and pleasant spirit. Those few minutes of your morning will set the mood for your entire wedding and I promise, you will look forward to your Wedding Dance and enjoy not only your First Dance, but the entire build-up towards your wonderful performance.

Your Wedding Day and Ceremony

You may agree with me that the day of your wedding is the most beautiful and exciting experience of your life. Everything being planned and coordinated to your needs and wishes: the amazing decorations, the food, the wedding cake, perfectly arranged sweetheart table, and every little detail is taken care of. The moments of your wedding ceremony are full of emotion, giving your parents, family, and friends an unconditional feeling of grace and love that will nourish them with the most cherished gift of all, the unforgettable memories.

After your magnificent ceremony, the wedding photos are taken while your guests enjoy the cocktail hour, followed by a wonderful evening full of speeches, dancing, and entertainment filled with beautiful moments of fun and enjoyment. After your photo session, the guests are welcome to take their seats while sharing the pleasant moments of your ceremony and looking forward to your grand entrance and most of all, "Your First Dance."

After your photoshoot and before your grand entrance, take a moment with your spouse in the Bride's room (a room in your venue assigned for the newlyweds) and watch your wedding routine one last time to get into the performance mood and get ready to start your future together with your first "Official" dance.

The Big Performance

The time has come, the moment you've worked so hard for is finally here: your long-awaited First Dance. You see the groomsmen and the bridesmaids lining up in front of you, preparing for the grand entrance, and you hear the chatter in the ballroom and literally feel the excitement of the wedding crowd as much as you can feel your own. Take a few deep breaths and imagine all the emotions and the joy you will bring while performing your Wedding Dance.

One of the most important things to remember when you walk into the ballroom and while performing is to look at your partner or the audience (depending on your choreography), but never onto the dance floor. If you perform your Wedding Dance nervous or anxious, thinking about how you look, how it turns out, or even what the guests will say about you and your performance, you will walk into a disaster. Let your muscle memory do the work for you and enjoy the once in a lifetime experience.

Your family and friends came to celebrate and enjoy the moments of your "Special Day" with you. Only you two know how much time and work you've put into your Wedding Dance, and the only thing you should think about is how much you enjoy your First ever Dance as husband and wife.

> *Remember, the secret is: This performance and the moments filled with all the little imperfections are creating and will become "Your Own Ultimate Wedding Dance!"*

Visual Examples of Dance Positions and Figures

Classic Position

Prom Position (Basic)

Prom Position (Holding Face)

Prom Position (With Kiss)

Prom Position (With Kiss - Holding Face)

Double Handhold Position (Basic)

Double Handhold Position (Double High Five)

One Handhold Position (Basic - Close to Each Other)

One Handhold Position (With High Five)

One Handhold Position (Basic - Far from Each Other)

One Handhold Position (Right to Right Hand)

Side by Side Position (Facing Audience)

Side by Side Position (With the Back to the Audience)

Visual Examples of Dance Positions and Figures

One Handhold Position
(Kissing the Bride's Hand)

Double Handhold Position
(Kissing the Bride's Hand)

The Gentlemen's Position
(Basic)

The Gentlemen's Position
(Hand behind the Back)

Double Handhold Position
(Bride in Front)

Basic Dip
(One Hand)

Basic Dip
(Both Hand)

Double Handhold Dip
(To the Left)

Double Handhold Dip
(To the Right)

Side by Side Position
(Groom Kneeling)

The Chair Position
(Hand on the Shoulder)

The Chair Position
(Holding Face)

Visual Examples of Dance Positions and Figures

The Underarm Turn
(Progression - from the Classic Position)

The Spot Turn
(Progression - from the Double Handhold Position)

The Slow Underarm Turn
(Progression - from the Side by Side Position)

The Roll-Out and Roll-In
(Progression - from the Double Handhold Position - Bride in Front)

Visual Examples of Dance Positions and Figures

The Walk-Around
(Progression - from the Side by Side Position)

The Walk-Around
(Progression - from the Side by Side Position - Groom Kneeling)

Walking Around Each Other
(Progression - from the Right to Right Side Position)

Visual Examples of Dance Positions and Figures

Classic Lift

Classic Lift
(Holding Face)

Deer Jump Lift
(One Arm Lift)

Deer Jump Lift
(Both Arms)

Face to Face Lift

Extended Face to Face Lift

Extended Face to Face Lift
(Holding Face)

Extended Face to Face Lift
(Spinning Progression)

Visual Examples of Dance Positions and Figures

The Spinning Face to Face Lift
(Progression - Spinning to the Groom's Left)

The Walking Deer Jump Lift
(Progression - Walking in a Straight Line)

The Turning Deer Jump Lift
(Progression - Turning to the Groom's Left)

The Spinning Face to Face Lift
(Progression - Spinning to the Groom's Left - the Bride's Arms on the Groom's Hips)

The Song Examples

*S*ong examples used for "The Classic" and the first part of "The Surprise Wedding Dance" and "The Entertainer":

- Come Away With Me by Norah Jones
- Can't Help Falling In Love With You by Elvis Presley
- Unchained Melody by The Righteous Brothers
- Perfect by Ed Sheeran
- A Thousand Years by Christina Perri
- First Day Of My Life by Bright Eyes (amazing lyrics)
- You Are The Best Thing by Ray LaMontagne
- Your Song by Ellie Goulding
- I'm Yours by Jason Mraz
- Let's Stay Together by Al Green
- All Of Me by John Legend
- Everything by Michael Bublé
- Bless The Broken Roads by Rascal Flatts
- Wonderful Tonight by Eric Clapton
- Say You Won't Let Go by James Arthur
- Because You Loved Me by Celine Dion
- Endless Love by Lionel Richie & Diana Ross
- Marry Me by Train
- Here Comes The Sun by The Beatles
- You Are The Reason by Leona Lewis & Calum Scott
- You Are So Beautiful by Joe Cocker
- God Gave Me You by Blake Shelton

and many more.

The Song Examples

Song examples used for the second part of "The Surprise Wedding Dance" and "The Entertainer":

- Proud Mary by Tina Turner (it has a slow and a fast part)
- Can't Stop The Feeeling by Justin Timberlake
- You Shock Me All Night Long by AC/DC
- Just The Way You Are by Bruno Mars
- I Want You To Want Me by Cheap Trick
- Walk This Way by Aerosmith. You may like the version with RUN DMC(badass song for Groom's solo)
- Are You Gonna Go My Way by Lenny Kravitz
- Happy by Pharrell Williams
- You Make My Dreams by Daryl Hall & John Oates
- Hey Ya by Outkast
- Shut Up And Dance by Walk The Moon
- I'm So Into You by Tamia

and many more.

Song Examples for The Bride's and Groom's Solo (you can use these songs for Bridesmaids and Groomsmen solos as well)

- Uptown Funk by Mark Ronson ft, Bruno Mars
- Shake It Off by Taylor Swift
- Put Some Sugar On Me by Def Leppard
- U Can't Touch This by MC Hammer
- Sexy And I Know It by Lmfao
- Firework by Katy Perry

and many more.

These are just a few songs of hundreds and thousands of songs you can find online that are suited for your First Dance, your solos and as background music.

Wedding Dance Guest Book

Guest Name _____

_____

_____

_____

Guest Name _____

_____

_____

_____

Guest Name _____

_____

_____

_____

Wedding Dance Guest Book

Guest Name _____

_____

_____

_____

Guest Name _____

_____

_____

_____

Guest Name _____

_____

_____

_____

Wedding Dance Guest Book

Guest Name _____

_____

_____

_____

Guest Name _____

_____

_____

_____

Guest Name _____

_____

_____

_____

Wedding Dance Guest Book

Guest Name _____

_____

_____

_____

Guest Name _____

_____

_____

_____

Guest Name _____

_____

_____

_____

Wedding Dance Guest Book

Guest Name _____

_____

_____

_____

Guest Name _____

_____

_____

_____

Guest Name _____

_____

_____

_____

Wedding Dance Guest Book

Guest Name _____

_____

_____

_____

Guest Name _____

_____

_____

_____

Guest Name _____

_____

_____

_____

Acknowledgements

The first thank you goes to my brother Michael. For all these years, he has had my back and I know I can count on him no matter where I am and what situations I am in. He always supports me and he is always there for me. I'm thankful for his excitement for life in general, his hard work and dedication that he carries with him since day one, but most of all his loyalty. And to his wife Martinka as well, you make my brother very happy.

To my Goddaughter, Alexandra and the light she shines everywhere she goes since the day she was born and for teaching me how to be a responsible Godfather.

To the most talented artist and awesome friend Yevgenia, for her friendship and artistic input that helped me throughout the process of writing and finishing this book and for the beautiful cover art.

To my dear British friends Stuart and Gina with the biggest hearts in the world and their amazing help and support, not only for this book, but for my artistry, and most of all, for their unconditional love since the day we met.

Thank you to my dear friend Lil for her wisdom and love. Her joy, enthusiasm and how she approaches life, teaches me how to live my life to the fullest.

My manager and awesome friend Rosee for her support and help in everything I set my mind to. Her dedication to help me and her faith in me gives me enormous strength.

Thank you to my friend Amber and her passion for her photography. Her energy is radiant and never ending.

My friends Dr. Michael and Dr. Barbara Grossman and their love for each other. Working with them gave me insight and valuable lessons for my work.

To my awesome buddy Dmitry and his professional work and expertise for the promotional video. Seeing you working gave me more motivation for my book.

To my actor friends KC and Carina for their patience on the set and their beautiful energy that made the day unforgettable.

To Cinzia, Gianni, Doriano and Delia, an amazing family that thought me what family is all about and supported me through my highs and lows in my dancing career. I will never forget that.

And last but not least, thank you to every wedding couple and all of you reading this book. I hope I have helped you with my knowledge and insight on the topics that you were unaware of and have inspired you with this book to open your mind about the First Dance and encouraged you to perform with passion and joy. I wish you a pleasant journey, not only with your Ultimate Wedding Dance, but your life journey as well.

Thank you

Sincerely Yours
Daniel

Made in the USA
Middletown, DE
02 November 2020